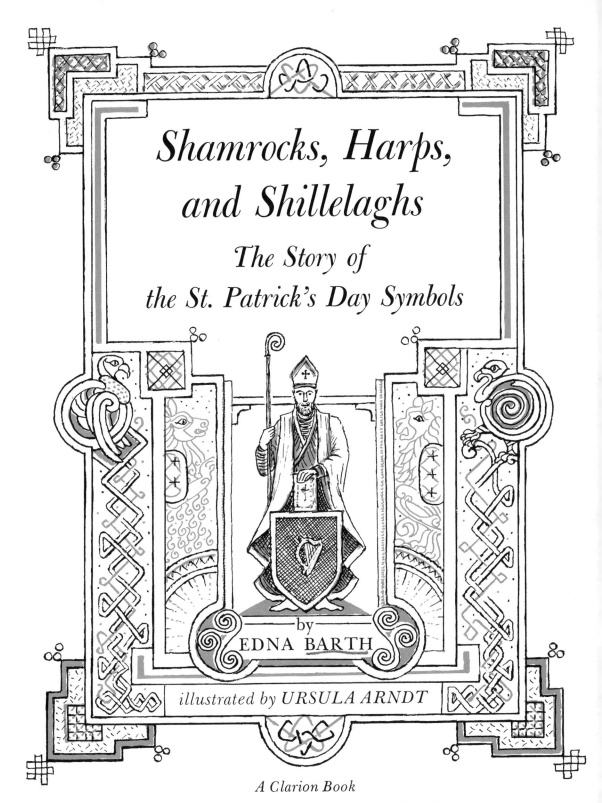

Shamrocks, Harps, and Shillelaghs

The Story of the St. Patrick's Day Symbols

by
EDNA BARTH

illustrated by URSULA ARNDT

A Clarion Book

THE SEABURY PRESS · NEW YORK

The author wishes to thank Ethna Sheehan and David C. Mercier for their help in locating some of the information in this book.

The Seabury Press,
815 Second Avenue, New York, New York 10017
Text copyright © 1977 by Edna Barth
Illustrations copyright © 1977 by Ursula Arndt
Printed in the United States of America

Library of Congress Cataloging in Publication Data
Barth, Edna.
Shamrocks, harps, and shillelaghs.
"A Clarion book."
Includes index and bibliography.
Summary: Explores the origin and meaning of the symbols and legends associated with St. Patrick's Day.
1. St. Patrick's Day—Juvenile literature.
[1. St. Patrick's Day] I. Arndt, Ursula. II. Title.
GT4995.P3B37   394.2′6   77-369   ISBN 0-8164-3195-7

Contents

OMETIME in February, the hearts and cupids of Valentine's Day give way to shamrocks and leprechauns, Irish harps, flags and shillelaghs, clay pipes and top hats. The color green floods the windows of card gifts, souvenirs, and decorations for holidays. shops, candy stores, and departments that sell St. Patrick's Day is coming.

For most Irish-Americans, this holiday is partly religious and partly festive. St. Patrick's Day church services are followed by parades and parties, Irish music, songs, and dances.

To other Americans, the festive side is the one that is known the best. Cheerfully noisy, greener than spring itself, the Irish holiday on March 17th is a welcome harbinger of the coming season.

St. Patrick's Day and its symbols are, in part, the story of the Irish and the land many of them left behind to come to the United States. For when they came, they brought with them their patron saint.

St. Patrick Himself

St. Patrick was a gentleman.
He came of decent people.
In Dublin town he built a church,
And on it put a steeple.
His father was a Callaghan,
His mother was a Brady,
His aunt was an O'Shaughnessy,
And his uncle was a Grady.

From *St. Patrick Was a Gentleman*

A song like this shows no disrespect for St. Patrick. Its familiar tone is a sign of affection. For the Irish feel very close to their saints, especially to St. Patrick.

Yet, strangely enough, the patron saint of Ireland was not Irish himself. It is thought that he was born in the British Isles. No one knows exactly where, but it may have been near the modern city of Dumbarton in Scotland. Exactly when St. Patrick lived is also uncertain. It was probably around 385–460 A.D.

Most of what is known about St. Patrick comes from his own *Confession,* written in his old age. In it there are few names and no dates. The *Confession* does tell us a good deal about his thoughts and feelings, though. So, as a person he is better known than most saints of those early years.

8

Three centuries before St. Patrick's time, the Roman Empire had conquered Britain. When Patrick was a boy, many of the people were Christians, living under Roman rule. The Roman Catholic religion, Roman customs, and Roman names all prevailed. The official language was Latin.

Patrick's father was an official who worked for the Roman government. He was known by the Roman name Calpurnius. The family's English name was Succat, meaning clever in war. Patrick's first name was Maewyn. In his writing, he spoke of himself as *patricius,* meaning well-born in Latin. Patrick is the English form of this word.

During Patrick's boyhood, the Roman Empire was near collapse and too weak to defend its holdings in distant lands. Britain became an easy prey for raiders, including those who crossed the Irish sea from the land the Romans called *Juverna.* In English this word was *Hibernia.*

The Irish raiders would land in their cowhide boats and creep up on a farm, looting and taking slaves.

When Patrick was sixteen, he was seized on his father's farm, bound, and carried off to Ireland. Some of the servants and perhaps Patrick's sisters were also taken. Their captors were sent by an important Irish chieftain or high king named Niall. Today, this old Irish name would be O'Neil.

In northern Ireland, in what is now Ulster, Patrick was sold to another chieftain named Miliuc. Much of his time after that was spent alone on the slopes of Slemish Mountain, tending his master's flocks of sheep. Lonely and homesick, he had plenty of time to think.

Before his capture, Patrick tells us in his *Confession,* he had broken God's Command-

ments and had paid little heed to the priests
who had tried to save him. His enslavement,
he believed, was a punishment—a punishment he well deserved.

During the long, lonely hours in the
fields and hills of Ireland, Patrick found comfort in praying. "I said a hundred prayers by
day and almost as many by night," he wrote.
"I arose before day, in the snow, in the frost,
and the rain, yet I received no harm."

Six years passed slowly by. Then in a
vision or dream, Patrick heard a voice saying,
"Thy ship is ready for thee." This was God's
way, he felt, of telling him to run away.

So he decided to act on the message and
headed for the sea coast, two hundred miles
away. There, as if by plan, was a ship that was
almost ready to set sail. Patrick begged to be
taken aboard, but was at first refused. Then
the captain changed his mind and took him
on as a member of the crew.

After a voyage of three days, the ship, with its cargo of Irish wolfhounds, landed somewhere in western Europe. Patrick and the others headed inland. For nearly a month they wandered through a barren, deserted area. Some of the men nearly died from exhaustion and hunger. Several of the dogs did starve to death along the way.

One day toward the end of their wanderings, when Patrick was praying for food, a herd of wild pigs came out of the woods. This was clearly a miracle, the sailors decided. And the miracle-maker should be kept as their slave. Once again Patrick had to make an escape.

Patrick and the sailors may have been in southern Gaul—what is now France. For around this time, the Vandals and other tribes invaded Gaul, burning and plundering the area.

From the time he escaped from his mates, St. Patrick devoted his life to God. His years of slavery had deprived him of the education he now wanted. Having much to make up, he studied for several years somewhere in Europe. No one is sure where.

After a few years, he tells us, he returned to his family, but only for a visit. While he was with his people, the visions began again. In one of these, Patrick heard "the voice of the Irish, crying as with one mouth, 'Come hither and walk among us.'"

This Patrick took as a command from God to return to Ireland. He was being called on, he felt, to convert the *pagans,* as the Christian church called people of other religions. So, leaving home, he set out to prepare himself still further in the monasteries of Europe. Just where he spent these years of study we do not know.

At this time, although the Roman Empire was near collapse, the Roman church was growing stronger. Missionaries were being

sent into pagan lands to convert people to the Christian faith. One of these lands was Ireland.

Having spent at least six years of his youth there, Patrick knew what he called "the land beyond which no man dwelt." He knew the manners, the customs, and language of the people who lived there. What was more, he had a deep urge to be the savior of a people who had once enslaved him.

It is known that, in 431 A.D., the Roman pope sent a bishop named Palladius to Ireland. Some say that Patrick knew this and was disappointed in not being sent instead. In any case, Palladius failed in his mission to Ireland. And, some time afterward, Patrick, now a bishop himself, set out with a group of companions for the land he had once fled.

The Irish, at this time, were still living in the Iron Age. Their plows, axes, and other tools were all made of iron. The people were *Celts*. Their ancestors had come to Ireland from western Europe hundreds of years before the birth of Christ.

What the Celts called their land we do not know. It may have been Erin. No one is

sure when this old Irish name came into use.
We do know that the country was first called
Ireland, or Irlanda, in the ninth century by in-
vaders from Scandinavia.

Living in clans or tribes, the Irish people
of St. Patrick's time hunted, fished, grew
crops, raised cattle, and made war on one another. Prisoners of war were used as slaves.
Wealth was reckoned in cattle.

Each tribe had its chieftain, a kind of
king. This king, in turn, paid tribute to a high
king, who was ruler of the province. And then
as now, Ireland was made up of four provinces
—Ulster, Munster, Leinster, and Connacht.

Below the king of an Irish tribe was a
class of landowners, who were like nobles.
The nobles fought for the king and granted
tracts of land to small farmers. In return, the
small farmer pledged loyalty to the landlord
and paid rent in the form of crops and cattle.

By St. Patrick's time, it is thought, some
of the Irish were already Christian. Most were
followers of the old pagan religion. The pagan
priests were known as *Druids* and also served
as teachers, judges, and magicians. The Druid
priests held ceremonies in sacred oak groves.
They worshipped nature gods, offered sacri-
fices, and foretold the future. Each chieftain
had his own Druid to give advice and protection by means of magic.

It is said that Patrick first landed in County Wicklow, south of what is now Dublin. He began preaching, but like Palladius before him, he was driven out of Wicklow.

With his companions, he then sailed northward toward the home of Miliuc, his former master. After many hardships and attempted landings, they finally reached the area. There, standing on a slope, Patrick saw Miliuc's house go up in flames.

How this happened is the subject of many legends. According to one story, Miliuc had heard of Patrick's coming and of the new religion's power. Rather than be put to shame by a former slave, he had set his house on fire and thrown himself into the flames.

As soon as possible, Patrick made his way to Tara, seat of Ireland's high kings. A pagan holiday was just beginning, perhaps *Beltane,* which was held around the first of May. At Beltane all lights were put out throughout the land. No one could light a fire until the king had lighted his on the hill of Tara. The reigning king at this time was Lagohaire, whose name today would be Leary.

Suddenly the flames of Patrick's campfires were seen on a slope across the river from Tara. Lagohaire was outraged. Jumping into his chariot, he hurried off with some Druids and high officials to Patrick's camp.

16

Out of fear of Patrick's magic, the Druids advised the king not to enter the camp grounds. Instead Patrick was told to come out. This Patrick did, saying, "Some put their faith in chariots and horses, others in God."

So the story goes. How much of it is truth and how much legend, no one knows. In any case, it is clear that Patrick was a tireless and fearless missionary. Moving from place to place, he preached to all who would listen, urging them to accept the Christian god.

Before long he was famous throughout Ireland. His nickname was Old Shaved Head. Some of the Irish made up this song about him:

17

Old Shaved Head cometh
Off the storm-tossed sea:
He wears a long robe,
A crooked staff hath he. . . .

Patrick would visit a chieftain and tell him about the new religion. He would recite from the Bible and describe the Christian heaven and hell. If the chieftain agreed to be baptized, it was usually easy to convince the rest of the tribe.

Finally, Patrick would ask for ground on which to build a church. When the ground was granted, he would mark off the church foundations with his staff. Then, leaving some monks behind to build the church, he would move on to a new area.

Patrick's missionary work was not always this easy. In fact, his life was in constant danger. On his travels, he never knew when an enemy might be lying in wait for him. At least once he was captured and held in irons by an angry chieftain.

Among his chief enemies were the Druids. Seeing the new religion as a threat, some of the Druids cast spells on Patrick and plotted to kill him. Other Druids were impressed by the Christian ideas and by Patrick's fervor. In time, they became Christians themselves. Some were ordained as priests.

Patrick never tried to stamp out old rites and customs. Instead, he found a way to combine them with Christian customs. The Irish had always honored their gods with spring fire rites, for example. So Patrick had the people gather outside the churches for Easter bonfires.

For thirty or forty years, Patrick labored among the Irish. In time, he traveled to Armagh in the province of Ulster. There, after baptizing Daire, the Armagh chieftain, he built a church on a height called The Ridge of Willow. Armagh became Patrick's home and the church center for all of Ireland.

Looking back in old age, Patrick felt pleased with his work. For a large part of Ireland was now Christian. He had not been seeking fame, but fame had come to him. Students were being sent to him from all over Europe.

When Patrick died, all of Ireland went into mourning. For twelve days the church elders prayed over his body. Later, people said that for all that time there was no night. Instead, the air was filled with a continual radiance. This was probably the light made by hundreds of candles and torches, for people came from far and near to pay their respects.

According to one tale, there was an argument after Patrick's death between the tribesmen of Armagh and those of Saul, where he had died. Both wanted him buried in their own area. To settle the argument, Patrick's

coffin was placed on a cart pulled by two wild oxen. The spot where they finally stopped would become Patrick's resting place. Patrick is said to have been buried at last near the River Quoile in Downpatrick, County Down, in Northern Ireland.

Like any leader who is loved and long remembered, Patrick was given credit not only for what he actually did but also for many other feats. It was said that he turned the Druids' fertile fields into bogs, took the fish from their rivers, and kept their kettles from ever boiling. As for the Druids themselves, he was supposed to have caused the earth to open up and swallow them.

He is also said to have caused the crippled to walk, the blind to see, and the deaf to hear. But best known of all is the legend that he drove the snakes out of Ireland.

What about the real St. Patrick? From his own *Confession* we know how brave, humble, and sincere he was. Until his coming, Ireland had no written history. The story of its past was told in the form of poems by the Irish bards. With St. Patrick and the Christian church came the Bible and other sacred books in the Latin language. This led to the art of reading and writing. In the monasteries built by Patrick and his successors, monks copied books by hand onto fine parchment. Often the pages were decorated with designs in gold, silver, and brilliant colors. One beautiful example is the eighth century *Book of Kells*.

This ancient book is on display in the library of Trinity College in Dublin.

Meanwhile, in much of Europe, civilization was close to collapse. Few learned to read and write. Most books that were written were of poor quality. The arts and crafts of the ancient world were largely forgotten. This time, beginning in the fifth century and lasting for six hundred years, is known as the Dark Ages.

Ireland, the only country to the west that had never come under Roman rule, kept Roman learning alive. In fact, Ireland became known as the "Island of Saints and Scholars."

Later on, during the Middle Ages, Irish monks often traveled to Rome. Some went as missionaries to parts of Italy and other countries. Today, in Belgium and France, as well as in Italy, there are shrines and churches dedicated to Irish saints. Among them is St. Patrick. The people honor him with no thought to his role as the patron saint of another nation.

St. Patrick's name is found all over Ireland today in the names of towns and villages like Kirkpatrick, Downpatrick, and Kilpatrick. And, dotting the countryside, are Patrick's Wells—streams and springs where Bishop Patrick is said to have baptized people.

Among the many churches that bear his

Dublin

New York City

name are a cathedral in Dublin and one in New York City. Patrick has long been a favorite name for boys, and not only in Ireland. Fitzpatrick, Kirkpatrick and such are common family names.

The Irish like to feel that their patron saint is their friend and protector. On Judgment Day, so a saying goes, all Irish people will be judged by St. Patrick, improving their chances of entering heaven.

The Irish not only honor their patron saint, they try to imitate him. In County Mayo there is a mountain called Croagh Patrick. Here, legend has it, the saint ordered all serpents out of Ireland. Here, too, he is said to have once spent the forty days of Lent, praying and fasting. Today, on the last Sunday in July, hundreds of people go as pilgrims to Croagh Patrick.

Another popular summer pilgrimage is to Patrick's Purgatory in County Donegal. There, on a small, stony island in Lough Derg, is an ancient shrine. People who had committed crimes once went there to do penance. Others went to fast and pray, as people do today.

For the past thousand years, Catholic saints have been chosen by authorities of the Catholic church. Before then, this was done

24

in a natural, informal way by the people themselves. All those who devoted their lives to religion were known as saints. One as outstanding as Bishop Patrick was revered long after his lifetime. This kind of person became a saint in a special sense.

Until 1969, the Catholic Church listed 350 saints. At that time, after a series of meetings known as Vatican II, Pope Paul VI approved cutting the number to 173. Among these are missionary saints, martyrs, defenders of the faith, and others of equal rank but different kind. St. Patrick is one of the missionary saints.

He is said to have divided those who devoted their lives to the church into three orders of saints. They were either "a glory on the mountaintop, a gleam on a hillside, or a faint light in a valley."

"A glory on the mountaintop" himself, St. Patrick is loved not only by the Irish. Saintly, yet human, he is loved by many others who have come to know him through stories and poems and through the celebration of St. Patrick's Day.

St. Patrick's Day Through the Centuries

At some time long ago, no one is sure when, a day was set aside in honor of St. Patrick. According to the custom of the times, this was not the saint's birthday but the day of his death—in our modern calendar, March 17th.

Besides being a religious holiday, St. Patrick's Day came to be thought of as the beginning of spring. Irish farmers usually planted their grain in March. Cattle were led out to summer pasture at about this time of year.

On St. Patrick's Day, Irish farmers would take a charred stick and mark a cross on the arm of each person in his family. As he did this, he would say, "In the name of the Father, the Son, and the Holy Ghost."

Later it became the custom to wear a sprig of shamrock on St. Patrick's Day. Some say this three-leaved plant was a symbol of the Father, Son, and Holy Ghost—the *trinity* of the Catholic faith.

In time, what had started out as a purely religious holiday in Ireland became part holy and part festive. In the morning everybody went to special masses in honor of the patron saint. In the afternoon, they paid visits to their friends and relatives. Some of the men gathered in the public houses to drink toasts to St. Patrick. People enjoyed singing and dancing.

As the centuries passed, St. Patrick's Day became more than a religious and festive holiday. It became a time for the Irish everywhere to show their unity.

From the twelfth century on, the Irish had struggled for independence from England as well as the right to their own religion. The day of their patron saint became a symbol of their survival and a time for expressing their feelings about Irish freedom. On the holiday, their national emblem, the shamrock, was worn proudly, sometimes in defiance of British rule.

Irish people came to America very early. Some claim that St. Brendan, a beloved Irish saint of the century after St. Patrick, was the first. St. Brendan is sometimes said to have explored eastern America one thousand years before Columbus.

Be that as it may, more than half of those who fought on the side of the colonies in the American Revolution were of Irish descent. Among the signers of the Declaration of Independence, there were more Irish than any others.

No wonder that St. Patrick's Day has been observed in America since colonial times. The first celebration outside of the church was held in Boston in 1737 by the Irish Charitable Society. The Friendly Sons of St. Patrick held celebrations in Philadelphia beginning in 1784. The New York group included Protestant as well as Catholic members. The first president was a Presbyterian.

In Ireland, meanwhile, hardships persisted and people continued to leave. Then came the potato famine of 1845–49. Hundreds of thousands fled to other countries. Hundreds of thousands of others died of starvation. By the end of the 1800s, a country of almost 9,000,000 had dwindled to half that number.

Of those who managed to leave Ireland, many settled in the United States. Coming from farms and with little education, they had few skills. Only the least desirable and poorest paying jobs were open to them. They dug ditches, labored on the railroads that were being built, worked in mills or as servants. To make ends meet, many Irish mothers were forced to take in other people's washing and ironing.

Like each new group of immigrants, the Irish were looked down on by many Americans who had once been newcomers themselves, or whose parents had. Sometimes this even included other Irish people.

And, like many other European immigrants in the United States, most of them were treated badly for being Catholics.

Aware of the bad feeling, and surrounded by strange customs, the Irish clung all the more tightly to their own. The feast day of their patron saint became a time for saying to the world, "We are Irish and we are proud of it." By the late 1800s there were St. Patrick's Day celebrations all across the United States.

Groups like The Friendly Sons of St. Patrick and the Ancient Order of Hibernians continued strong. New ones like the St. Patrick's Benevolent Society of Los Angeles sprang up. Such groups were the sponsors of the celebrations. In New York, Philadelphia, Boston, Los Angeles, and many other cities, St. Patrick's Day became the big national day for the Irish.

Special St. Patrick's Day masses were followed by parades, luncheons, banquets, toasts, and speeches. In Irish homes there were festive dinners. The evening was devoted to Irish music, pageants, plays, and dancing. People, young and old, wore something green, and on display everywhere were the shamrock and the green Irish flag with the gold harp of Tara on it.

Today, in the United States, there are more people of Irish descent than there are in Ireland. St. Patrick's Day is celebrated much as it was a hundred years ago. The Irish who are Catholics may attend special masses. In the afternoon there is almost always a parade. In the evening there are dinners and dances, or celebrations in people's homes.

The holiday events begin a week or two before St. Patrick's Day. Irish clubs hold banquets, luncheons, dinners, dances, and parties. Sometimes they honor Irish-Americans who are stars in show business or other fields. Entertainers, some of them straight from Ireland, go on tour.

A new feature in recent years is the Irish fortnight. For two weeks certain colleges and universities have special Irish programs. They feature Irish poets, fiddlers, singers, dancers, and actors. Scholars give lectures on Irish history and folklore. Everyone is invited, and many of the programs are free.

In Ireland, people used to say, "St. Patrick's Day, we'll all be gay." Masses and parades were followed by dancing, singing, and drinking. Hardworking, downtrodden people forgot their troubles for an evening.

Frowned upon by Ireland's government and churches, this kind of celebration has been discouraged in recent years. Today there is more stress on the holy side. St. Patrick's Day is a legal holiday in Ireland. Schools, post offices, and banks are closed. Churches are jammed with people wearing sprigs of shamrock. A hymn sung in many churches is *St. Patrick's Breastplate,* sometimes said to have been written by the saint himself.

In many Irish towns, St. Patrick's Day plays and concerts are performed in the afternoon. School children often take part in special programs. Some of the hotels feature dancing to Irish music for people who have come to Ireland for the holiday. And nearly everywhere there are parades.

Another feature of St. Patrick's Day in Ireland is the old Gaelic sport of hurling. Something like the modern game of field hockey, hurling is played with curved sticks just as hockey is. The ball may be batted either over or under the goal posts. On the holiday, the Railway Cup hurling final takes place. The two provinces that have reached the final now compete for the cup. Both hurling teams dress in green.

In most of Ireland, there are no television programs until about 5 P.M. On St. Patrick's Day, they begin earlier. Some are based on the life of St. Patrick. Some present the music of a famous Irish composer, such as Seán O'Riada. Others feature the traditional Irish music that is as popular in Ireland as country and western music is in the United States today.

Cead mile failte! is Gaelic for "A hundred thousand welcomes!"

In the Irish countryside, March 17th is a day when friends and relatives visit one another. Those who know Gaelic, the old Irish tongue, exchange greetings in it.

Gaelic, the language of Celtic tribes who settled in Ireland long ago, had been spoken there since the beginning of Irish history. Then, in modern times, English took the place of Gaelic in most of Ireland. Gaelic was in danger of dying out, but it is now being taught along with English in Irish schools.

One Gaelic greeting that might be heard on St. Patrick's Day goes like this: *Dia's Muire dhuit*—God and Mary be with you.

The other person replies: *Dia's Muire agus Padraig dhuit*—God and Mary and Patrick be with you.

Heard all over Ireland on St. Patrick's

Day are the rollicking strains of the national anthem. This is *Amran na bFiann,* meaning "A Soldier's Song." It is almost always sung in Gaelic. With its lively march tune, it is often played by military bands in parades.

Carried in parades and waving from public buildings in towns and cities is the green, white, and orange flag of Ireland. And, in city and country alike, sprigs of shamrock are pinned to hats and lapels. For the "wearin' of the green" is another sign that St. Patrick's Day is a national as well as a religious holiday.

The Wearin' of the Green

Most holidays that we celebrate have their special colors. As everyone knows, red and green stand for Christmas, and black and orange for Halloween. When the red and pink of Valentine's Day disappear, there is a burst of refreshing green—the color of Ireland and of St. Patrick's Day.

Wherever greeting cards or party goods are sold, we see green flags, banners, and shillelaghs, green party hats and streamers, green shamrocks and carnations of cloth or paper. As March 17th draws closer, florists' windows fill with green carnations and pots of Irish shamrocks.

On the holiday itself, whether Irish or not, many Americans wear something green. It might be a green dress, sweater, skirt, shirt, or pants, a green tie, scarf, hat, or socks.

In Ireland, many little girls wear green hair ribbons on St. Patrick's Day. Some of the boys wear a green badge with a golden harp on it. And, of course, young and old wear sprigs of shamrock.

On St. Patrick's Day in 1959, President Sean O'Kelly of the Republic of Ireland came to Washington, D.C. A long green carpet awaited him at the airport. His host, President Eisenhower, wore a green necktie. Other officials had on green socks. In the United States Congress, which he visited, the Irish president saw a green carnation in every lapel.

At dinner that evening, the guest of honor spoke his mind. So much green gave him mixed feelings, he confessed. For, along with its happy reminders, the color green made him think of the many tragic events in his nation's past.

Back in the twelfth century, with the approval of the Catholic pope, King Henry II of England had set out to conquer and convert Ireland. The invaders he sent were Normans, descendants of men from Normandy who had conquered England the century before. King Henry rewarded the Normans with large tracts of land taken from the Irish. There the Normans settled, building castles. The ruins of some of these are still standing.

As time went on, the Normans mixed with the Irish, adopting Irish customs and speaking Gaelic. Many joined forces with the Irish to fight the British. By the 1400s, the only region still held by the English was an area around Dublin called "The Pale."

In the 1500s things were different, for England had grown much more powerful. English explorers were claiming territory throughout the world. English trading ships were sailing the seven seas.

Breaking from the Church of Rome, King Henry VIII declared himself head of the Anglican or English church. He closed all the churches and monasteries in Ireland and put a ban on the Catholic religion. Yet most of the Irish remained Catholic.

In the 1600s English rule grew still more severe. The Irish rebelled, but each rebellion was put down. By the middle of the century, nine-tenths of the country was owned by Protestants.

Then, in 1685 James II, a Catholic himself, came to the British throne. The Irish took hope. But in a few years James was ousted by the British nobles who wanted England to remain Protestant. Fleeing to France, James was given French money and arms, and went on to Ireland.

There, William of Orange, James's Protestant son-in-law, defeated him at the famous battle of the Boyne in 1690. The treaty of peace promised land to the Irish Catholics as well as more freedom.

This promise was broken, though, and Ireland remained under Protestant rule. Most of the Irish remained faithful to the Catholic religion, however. For this they paid dearly under the Penal Laws that soon followed. Irish Catholics were forbidden to own or rent land, to vote, or hold office. Nor did they have a voice in the British Parliament, where the laws were made.

Catholic churches, monasteries, convents, and schools were closed once more. Priests and nuns were banned, so Catholic masses had to be held in secret. "Hedge schoolmasters"

taught reading and writing, sometimes even Greek and Latin, behind the hedges on country roads.

The harsh laws continued for more than a century. Then, in 1776 an Englishman threw the House of Lords into an uproar when he introduced a bill that would make it lawful for an Irish Catholic to rent a cabin and potato patch. But the American colonies had broken away from England, and most of Ireland sided with them. So, in order to keep Ireland under control, the English now gave Irish Catholics the right to hold land.

In 1801 Ireland was made a part of the United Kingdom of Great Britain. Again hopes for peace and freedom arose, but to no avail. Not until 1829 did Irish Catholics win the right to hold office. And for thirty years more the Church of England remained Ireland's official church.

After the famine of the 1840s, those who remained in Ireland continued to chafe under British rule. Groups like the *Fenians* began forming. Some had branches in America as well as in Ireland. Catholic or Protestant, they wanted Ireland for the Irish.

Ireland's patron saint became a symbol of Irishness. St. Patrick's Day became a time for expressing Irish unity and fighting spirit.

Ireland's national color was, at one time, St. Patrick's blue. By the nineteenth century, the color green had taken its place. During Queen Victoria's reign, her Irish regiments were forbidden to "wear the green," meaning to display the shamrock on St. Patrick's Day.

From this came *The Wearin' of the Green,* the song that begins:

> Oh, Paddy dear! and did ye hear the news
> that's going 'round?
> The Shamrock is forbid by law to grow
> on Irish ground!
> No more St. Patrick's Day we'll keep; his
> color can't be seen,
> For there's a cruel law again' the Wearin'
> o' the Green!

Long before St. Patrick, the green of grass, of shamrocks, and of all growing things had special meaning to the Irish. It was a symbol of springtime. At this time of the year, like other people of ancient times, the Irish honored the gods and goddesses of plant life. Then with the coming of St. Patrick and other missionaries, some of the old pagan rites became linked to important days in the Christian calendar. Gradually, Easter and St. Patrick's Day took the place of the ancient pagan celebration of springtime.

40

In the mild climate of Ireland, spring is well along by March 17th.

> "As the sturgeon or salmon swim exactly
>   in midstream,
> So does St. Patrick's Day fall exactly in
>   midspring."

This is a Gaelic saying handed down from long ago. Another saying goes like this:

> "St. Patrick's Day turns the warm side of
>   the stone uppermost."

Covered with green valleys, fields, and pastures, Ireland is known as The Emerald Isle. Making the green seem even greener is the gray stone of old walls, rugged mountains, and ruined castles, towers, churches, and cottages.

In the language of colors, green stands for nature. Green also stands for hope! The green of St. Patrick's Day reminds us that the heroic Irish have sometimes survived on little more than hope.

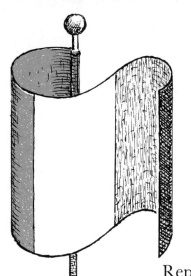

Green, White, and Orange

Three vertical stripes, one green, one white, and one orange—the flag of the Republic of Ireland. The Irish tricolor is carried in St. Patrick's Day parades in Dublin, Los Angeles, Atlanta, New York City, Montreal, Sydney, Australia, or almost any town or city where people of Irish descent live.

The green stands for the Gaelic and Catholic majority of the Emerald Isle. The orange is for Ireland's Protestants. The white is a symbol of the wish for peace between the two.

An old Irish pledge of allegiance went like this:

> We are willing to fight for the flag that we
>   love,
> Be the chances great or small.
> We are willing to die for the flag above,
> Be the chances nothing at all.

Irish history is filled with times when people did indeed fight and die for their flag, the symbol of their nation. The colors of today's Irish flag were used by the militant

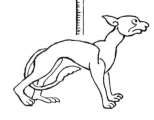

Young Ireland movement in 1848, but in reverse order, with the orange first. Like the tricolor of the French Revolution of 1789, it stood for liberty, equality, and brotherhood.

By the twentieth century, the Irish were represented in the British House of Commons. The worst laws imposed on Irish Catholics were gone. Yet most people still had to scratch a living out of small patches of land and pay rents to English landlords.

In the last decades of the nineteenth century, a movement toward Home Rule or self-government had begun. In 1906 some of the Irish who favored Home Rule formed a group called *Sinn Fein,* meaning We Ourselves. They and other groups stirred up a spirit of Ireland for the Irish.

Northern Ireland, made up mostly of descendants of Scottish settlers, wished to remain with Great Britain. In the North, linen mills and shipyards had been started. Since these depended on trade with Britain, the North had a different view of the ruling country. Feeling against Home Rule ran strong there.

The North was mostly Protestant, too, while the South was mostly Catholic. Of course, this served to divide Ireland still further.

A corps of volunteer soldiers was formed in the North to resist Home Rule—by force if necessary. The South's reply was a corps of volunteers of its own. When all this was at the boiling point, World War I broke out. The Home Rule bill was put aside.

But the issue remained alive. In Easter Week of 1916, more than a thousand Irish men rose up against British rule. They seized buildings in Dublin and held them for a week. Then, forced to surrender, they were jailed or deported. Fifteen of their leaders were executed.

During this Easter Week Rebellion, the green, white, and orange flag became a symbol of Free Ireland.

At the next election, 73 of the 105 Irish seats in the House of Commons were won by the Irish Home Rule Party, the Sinn Fein. The new members refused to go to the British Parliament in England. Instead they set up a parliament of their own in Dublin called the *Dail*. For protection, they formed a military wing, the Irish Republican Army.

Finally in 1921 a treaty was signed with Britain. By its terms, the Irish Free State was established. While still a member of the British Commonwealth, the new Irish state was self-governing.

There were twenty-six counties in the Irish Free State. The other six counties in the Northeast became Northern Ireland, which would continue as a part of the United Kingdom.

In 1937 the Irish Free State adopted a new constitution and changed its name to *Eire,* the ancient Gaelic name for all of Ireland. The green, white, and orange flag became official.

In 1948 Eire withdrew from the British Commonwealth and became the Republic of Ireland. The tricolor became the republic's flag.

Northern Ireland, as part of the United Kingdom, uses the British flag. A combination of English, Scottish, and Irish symbols, it has red crosses with white borders on a blue background.

On St. Patrick's Day, in the Republic of Ireland, the flag that is carried in parades is the green, white, and orange tricolor.

Seen more often in the United States on this holiday is a small, green flag with a gold harp on it. Not a true flag, this is an emblem of Ireland and the Irish.

Either flag serves to remind us that St. Patrick's Day is a patriotic as well as a religious holiday.

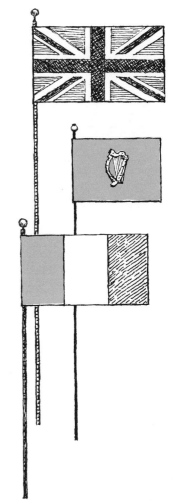

45

The Irish Shamrock

In the language of symbols, a heart pierced with an arrow stands for Valentine's Day. A green wreath with a red bow stands for Christmas. A grinning jack-o'-lantern stands for Halloween. For St. Patrick's Day, a single symbol sums things up: a green shamrock. A small, three-leaved plant known as a trefoil, it looks something like our clover.

For centuries the shamrock has been an emblem of St. Patrick as well as of Ireland. With the English rose and the Scottish thistle, it appears on the coat of arms of Great Britain.

Shamrock is the English name for the plant known in Gaelic as *seamrog*. Exactly what a true Irish shamrock is has sometimes been debated. An Englishman once claimed that it was the wood sorrel. A loyal Irishman wrote a letter to a newspaper, the *Dublin Penny Journal*. He called the wood sorrel "that sour, puny plant" and the Irish shamrock "our little darling." The same man claimed that when St. Patrick drove the snakes out of Ireland, he was standing in a patch of shamrock.

46

One sentimental Irish song gives the saint credit for having brought it to Ireland.

> There's a dear little plant that grows in
>   our Isle
> 'Twas St. Patrick himself sure that set it.
> And the sun on his labor with pleasure
>   did smile,
> And with dew from his eye often wet it.
> It shines through the bog, through the
>   brake, through the mireland,
> And he called it the dear little shamrock
>   of Ireland.

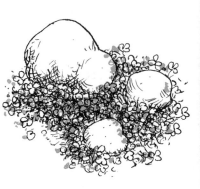

The mild, misty Irish climate keeps the shamrock fresh and green, winter and summer. Its seed is everywhere. As an Irishman once said, "Drop some lime or limestone gravel on the top of a bare mountain or into a bog, and up springs a shamrock."

When the Irish first displayed the shamrock in honor of their patron saint is uncertain. Some say that St. Patrick himself used the three-leaved plant as a symbol of the *trinity*.

This may be only another legend. However, St. Patrick does mention the trinity very often in his writing. And *St. Patrick's Breastplate,* the hymn he is sometimes said to have written, speaks of "Three in One, and One in Three." With shamrocks growing all over

47

Ireland, it seems natural for Bishop Patrick to have used it to teach the idea of the trinity.

Long before Patrick's time, the number three had a special place in far older religions. Among the Druids, three was the number of their unknown god. The ancient Romans believed the world was ruled by three gods: Jupiter, king of the heavens, Neptune, king of the seas, and Pluto, king of the earth or Underworld.

In Greek myths three is a magical number. There are Three Graces, for instance, and Three Fates. The Greek scholar Pythagoras said the number three stood for completeness—something with a beginning, a middle, and an end.

It is not surprising that the number three, with its long history, found a place in the Christian religion. It also found its way into folk and fairy tales. For as everyone knows, there are often three sisters, three brothers, three tasks, or three wishes.

And there have been all sorts of sayings about this number. "Never two without three," for instance, meaning three disasters or three pieces of good luck.

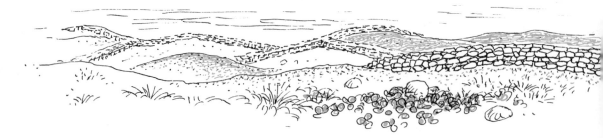

The strange importance of the number three may have come from the awe that people felt before the mystery of birth. Two animals or human beings mated, and behold, a third life came into being. Before conception and birth were understood, this must have seemed like something magical.

A symbol of St. Patrick at first, the shamrock became, in time, a symbol of the way the Irish felt about their country. In 1777, it was used as an emblem by the Irish "volunteers," as the British called the Irish regiments in their army. Later, it became an emblem of rebellion. When Queen Victoria forbade her Irish soldiers to display the shamrock, it became more than ever a national symbol.

The shamrock still grows freely all over Ireland. In some areas, people gather it in large quantities from fields and meadows in early March. By St. Patrick's Day, shamrocks by the millions are shipped all over the world.

A certain town in Florida is called Shamrock. Many people send St. Patrick's Day cards or letters there to be postmarked.

Cheerful, decorative, rich in history, the shamrock is probably the best known and most popular of all the symbols of the Irish holiday.

St. Patrick and the Serpents

Then success to bold Saint Patrick's fist.
He was a Saint so clever.
He gave the snakes and toads a twist,
And banished them forever.

The thing that almost everyone remembers best about St. Patrick is the saying "He drove the snakes out of Ireland." Pictures of the saint often show him in the act, a sprig of shamrock in his hand.

An old legend tells of one stubborn serpent who refused to go. Making a box, St. Patrick invited the serpent to get inside.

"It's too small for me," said the serpent.

"No, indeed," said St. Patrick. "It's just right for you."

They argued some more. Then the serpent said, "I still say it's too small, and I'll prove it."

With that, he climbed into the box; St. Patrick slammed down the lid and heaved the whole thing into the ocean.

In another legend, St. Patrick scared the snakes by beating a drum. Beating a little too hard, he knocked a hole in the drum, but an angel appeared and quickly mended it for him.

51

Still another legend, told here and there in Ireland, concerns a monster serpent living in a mountain lake. "Between you and me," St. Patrick told the monster, "I have so many other serpents to banish that I'll have to ask you to wait here until tomorrow."

When the next day came with no sign of St. Patrick, the serpent called out, "Is it tomorrow yet? Is it tomorrow?"

Since tomorrow never comes, the poor serpent can still be heard crying out today— or so people living near the lake like to pretend.

Some legends claim that St. Patrick made the Irish soil so distasteful to serpents that they die if they even touch it. Bede, an eighth century English scholar, went still further. He said the first whiff of Irish air would kill a snake sailing aboard a ship that was bound for Ireland.

Centuries later, in 1831, a man in Ireland decided to find out if it was true that snakes hated Irish soil or Irish air. He bought six harmless snakes in London, took them home, and let them loose.

A week later, one of the snakes was found a few miles away. Thinking the snake was an unusual kind of eel, the finder showed it to a scientist. He was told that he had found, not a rare fish, but a common garden snake.

Since this happened a few miles from the spot where St. Patrick was buried, alarming rumors spread. Some thought that the world was about to end.

Those who knew better were angry to think that someone had brought snakes into the country. For Ireland really is free of snakes. As far back as one can trace, they have never been native to this island country. The only reptiles there are lizards.

Why St. Patrick is given the credit for getting rid of the snakes has never really been answered. One Irish poet suggests an interesting explanation. In the eighth century, Ireland was invaded by Norsemen from Scandinavia, he begins. The Norse word for toad was *paud*. A famous man that the Norsemen heard about was called *Paudrig*—which is how the name Patrick sounded to them. The Norsemen took this to mean *expeller of toads*. Finding few toads in Ireland, they decided that Paudrig must have expelled them along with snakes, which they never seemed to encounter at all.

The belief that St. Patrick had banished

PAUDRIG

the snakes is very old. Perhaps in those early times, people in Ireland reasoned something like this: Ireland was a Christian country. It was also free of snakes. St. Patrick, who had wiped out the old pagan religion must have also expelled the snakes, a symbol of evil.

A Sprig of Shillelagh

Oh! An Irishman's heart is as stout as
    shillelagh,
It beats with delight to chase sorrow or
    woe;
When the piper plays up, then it dances
    as gaily,
And thumps with a whack to leather a
    foe.

The *shillelagh* is the old Irish word for a
short, stout, oak club or cudgel. As a symbol
of the Irish, it has a place in St. Patrick's Day.

Shillelagh was the name of a famous oak
forest that once stood in County Wicklow. A
club or cudgel cut from one of the oaks was
known as a "sprig of shillelagh." Later, the
name was given to any cudgel made of oak.

A man in Dublin once said that the Irish
of early times must have lived "under the
greenwood tree." As proof, he pointed out
that an Irishman would not walk or wander
without a shillelagh. Away from home, he
would beg, borrow, or steal one. In a game of
hurling, he played with a shillelagh. At a fair
or market, he wouldn't buy or sell without the
stout oak stick in his hand.

Ancient feuds between families or different parties were often fought out with shillelaghs at county fairs. Irish novels of the eighteenth century frequently describe this. Only later, after the Irish were drawn together by a national spirit, did such feuding end.

Meanwhile, under the Penal Laws, England robbed many landowners of their estates. The oaks of Shillelagh and trees of all kinds were soon chopped down. The timber was sold in England. A country that had once been known as "The Wooded Isle" became so bare and treeless that people began to cut and burn turf or peat to use as fuel. Today, most Irish homes are still heated with some form of turf.

oak

Blackthorn

Oak was especially scarce. An Irishman was now more likely to cut his club or walking stick from a blackthorn hedge. The true shillelagh became a thing of the past.

In the United States and in Ireland, in the nineteenth or twentieth century, a kind of stage Irishman was born. Dressed in the style of the Irish countryside, he sang Irish airs, swinging a shillelagh to add a flourish.

A real shillelagh was never swung, but grasped in the middle. A fighter used two. With one hand he dealt a blow. With the other, he warded off the "whack" of his opponent.

Today, tourists bring back mock shillelaghs made of blackthorn bound with green ribbons as souvenirs of the Emerald Isle. In St. Patrick's Day parades, officials in top hats often carry blackthorn walking sticks. Children on the sidelines, some of them only toddlers, clutch toy shillelaghs made of green plastic. All are symbols of the staunch spirit of the Irish.

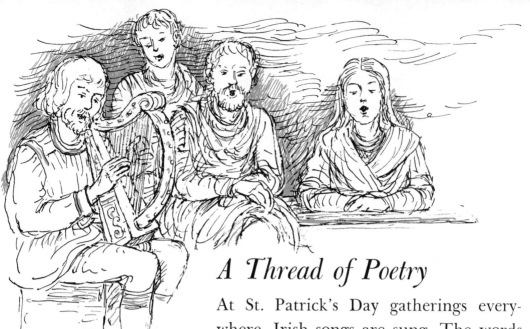

A Thread of Poetry

At St. Patrick's Day gatherings everywhere, Irish songs are sung. The words and music, like the history of Ireland, range from sad and sorrowful to lively and lilting. Many of the songs, like *The Harp That Once Through Tara's Halls* or *Danny Boy,* are old Irish airs. The words were written by Irish poets of the past one hundred fifty years.

Much of what we know of Ireland in St. Patrick's time is due to the bards or poets of those early days. Before Ireland had a written language, tales of bygone days were recited by poets, with harp music in the background.

Anything worthy of being remembered was put into verse. This might be the laws the Irish lived by, or the history of a leading family, or the deeds of champions.

The oldest Irish poems are said to be those of Ossian, who told of the third century hero Finn MacCool. A bit from one of Ossian's poems, translated into English, goes like this:

58

A tale for you: oxen lowing, winter snow-
    ing; summer passed away.
Wind from the north, high and cold; low
    the sun and short his course;
wildly towing the waves of sea.
The fern burns deep red; men wrap
    themselves closely; the wild
goose raises her wonted cry; cold seizes
    the wing of the bird: 'tis
the season of ice, sad my tale.

In St. Patrick's time, the Irish lived by
what are called the Brehon laws. It is said that
Bishop Patrick was asked to put these into
proper order. He did so, the account goes on,
and then had a poet "throw a thread of poetry
around them."

Old Irish legends tell of St. Patrick's love
of listening to Irish hero tales. The bard
Caoilte so enchanted Patrick that it seemed
sinful, and he confessed this weakness to his
guardian angel. However, the angel approved
of Caoilte's poems, so Patrick ordered that
they be written down for Irish people of the
future.

For Caoilte himself and other poets, St.
Patrick made two wishes. Every third word
they uttered should be full of melody. And
every poet should be the highlight of any
gathering and the equal of any king.

In St. Patrick's time, poets did in fact rank next to kings. At the table, a poet was entitled to the "King's joint"—the best haunch of meat. His honor price, if anyone wronged him, was twenty-one cows, the same as a king's. His person was, if anything, more sacred.

Each one was usually the official poet for a certain king or chieftain. In return for his services, the poet was given a house, land, cattle, horses, hounds, servants, and slaves. Held in fear and awe, he was protected by law, even outside his own territory.

So poets traveled about a good deal, visiting the homes of important people. There, the poets and their attendants enjoyed every comfort and luxury. In return, the poets were expected to sing the praises of their hosts.

A poet who was not satisfied might recite poems filled with jibes and insults. His host would be disgraced before his friends and family.

Some of the poets made the most of this. Where the living was most comfortable, they often settled in for weeks or even months.

A hundred years or so after St. Patrick's time, the poets had become a great burden to rich households. They were now in danger of being banished.

It was Saint Columcille, sometimes known as St. Columba, who saved them. He convinced an assembly of kings, nobles, scholars, and churchmen that they could not do without their poets. So Ireland continued as a land where poetry flourished. A few centuries later, one poet wrote these charming lines:

> A hedge of trees surrounds me
> A blackbird's lay sings to me;
> Above my lined booklet
> The trilling birds chant to me.
> In a grey mantle from the tops of bushes
> The cuckoo sings;
> Verily—may the Lord shield me!—
> Well do I write under the greenwood.

As time went on, Ireland became a center for the training of poets. Students came from England, Scotland, and Wales, as well as from western Europe. At special schools for bards, they studied for as long as twelve years.

The bardic schools continued into the seventeenth century. The poetry they produced has helped keep the Irish in touch with their own history.

Then came the law forbidding education for Irish Catholics. Those who wished to learn went secretly to the illegal "hedge schools." Taught mostly without books, the students stored what they learned in their memories. A good deal of this was poetry.

The hedge schoolmaster might be a poet or scholar. He might be the son or grandson of a graduate of a bardic school. Often, through him, a love of poetry was handed down.

At last in 1831, the British set up free elementary schools in Ireland. The teaching was done in English.

The famine of the 1840s killed many of the Irish who still spoke Gaelic. Many others who knew the language left Ireland. The Irish who remained were losing touch with their own tongue—the main link with their country's past.

By the end of the nineteenth century, the Irish language had all but died out. Once known for its poets and storytellers, Ireland was almost silent.

Some of the remaining poets and scholars found this alarming. The Irish, they felt, should be aware of their proud history. They should be acquainted with the Irish language, Irish poetry, art, and music. With this in mind, they formed the Gaelic League.

Soon people of all classes in Dublin were learning Gaelic. Many young people spent their spare time learning native Irish dances and folk songs. Some took to making and wearing clothes with a Celtic look.

THE ABBEY THEATRE

James Joyce

Lady Gregory

W. B. Yeats

J. M. Synge

Sean O'Casey

Old Irish legends, poems, and ballads were brought to light. Soon people were singing the ballads and telling the stories. All this helped to rebuild a pride in being Irish.

As Ireland awakened, literary talents awakened too. Poets, playwrights, and novelists began writing in a new, more hopeful spirit. In Dublin, the Abbey Theatre came into being in 1904. There, plays by and about the Irish were performed.

Within twenty-five years, it was said that Ireland had more important writers than any country in the world. Lady Gregory, J. M. Synge, James Joyce, W. B. Yeats, Sean O'Casey, and Padraic Colum were but a few of these.

Yeats, a leader in the Gaelic revival, is one of the great poets of this century. He is also known for the Irish folk and fairy tales that he collected and retold. One of his special interests was in fairies and ghosts.

64

Padraic Colum, another gifted poet, was also intensely interested in folk tales and gathered many that had been handed down among the Irish people. In 1914, he came to the United States. Here he taught at Columbia University, lectured, and translated Irish tales for children.

Padraic Colum

Today the Irish are known for their fresh, poetic way of talking and writing—and no wonder. It is part of a long tradition. And St. Patrick's Day reminds us that life in the United States is richer for this.

> I arise today
> Through the strength of heaven:
> Light of sun,
> Radiance of moon,
> Splendour of fire,
> Speed of lightning,
> Swiftness of wind,
> Depth of sea,
> Stability of earth,
> Firmness of rock.
>
> From *St. Patrick's Breastplate*

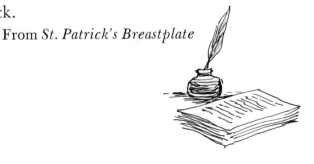

The Harp That Once Through Tara's Halls

The shape of a harp might not, in itself, suggest St. Patrick's Day. But if a harp is colored green and gold or shown with a sprig of shamrock, it quickly becomes a symbol of this Irish holiday. Like the shamrock, it is a symbol of Ireland itself.

One of the oldest of musical instruments, the harp has been important to the Irish from earliest times. Long before they had a written history, it played a part in their myths and legends.

In one Irish myth, the harp was owned by the Dagda, highest of the Divine Folk. He alone could call forth its various moods—joy, sorrow, or repose.

Envious of the Dagda, the powers of cold and darkness managed to steal the harp and hide it in their fortress. So the god of light and the god of art were sent to the land of cold and darkness to rescue the harp. With great struggle, they made their way into the chilly fortress.

There, on the wall, hung the sacred harp. By repeating the harp's two secret names, the young gods were able to seize it and carry it off.

With their return, the Dagda held a council of the Divine Folk and played the harp for them. He called a wail strain to make them weep, a smile strain to make them joyful, and then a sleep strain. At that, the whole company fell into a blissful sleep.

Among the ancient Norse people who lived in what is now Norway, Sweden, and Denmark, the harp stood for a mystic ladder between heaven and earth. No wonder that in many Norse tales, a hero asks that his harp be buried with him.

In the Middle East, there was once a country called Mesopotamia. Stone carvings found there show that harps were in use as early as three thousand years before Christ.

In ancient Egypt, harps had an important role. In the tomb of King Rameses II, for instance, large harps are shown in wall paintings. This was twelve hundred years before Christ.

The ancient Hebrews used harp music in their religious ceremonies.

Many other groups who lived around the Mediterranean Sea in ancient times also had harps of various kinds and sizes. The Greeks and Romans were exceptions. The lyre and cithara were more common with them.

Irish stone carvings and metal work of early Christian times show people playing harps. This is one of the ways we know that harp music was popular at the time of St. Patrick.

Among the Irish kings and nobles of the day, music and storytelling were the chief indoor amusement. As a poem was recited in honor of the head of the household, the drawn-out strains of the harp formed a pleasant accompaniment.

The old Irish harp, the *clarsach,* was small, with a sound box carved from one solid block of wood. The harper held it on his knee, plucking the thick, brass strings with the long fingernails of the other hand. The music had a ringing, bell-like sound.

The clarsach was quite different from the modern harp, which is larger with a shallow sound box and foot pedals that help control the strings.

One well-known Irish song of modern times is *The Harp That Once Through Tara's Halls.* The words were written by Thomas Moore, an Irish Poet. The first stanza goes like this:

> The harp that once through Tara's halls,
> The soul of music shed,
> Now hangs as mute on Tara's walls
> As if that soul were fled.

Tara is a hill in County Meath, twenty miles northeast of Dublin. Here, until the year 560, stood the hall of the Irish kings. And here in early Christian times, kings, churchmen, princes, and bards gathered. To the strains of harp music, the bards recited the chronicles of Ireland.

The silent harp of the song is a sad reminder that we can never really know what that music was like. Some of the ancient bardic poems were written down, but the music was not.

For many years the harp was the only instrument of any importance in Ireland. When the Normans came there in the twelfth century, they rated Irish harpists and harp music far above those of France, England, or Wales. Sir Francis Bacon of England once said, "No harp hath a sound so melting." Men from Scotland and western Europe were sent to Ireland to be trained in harp playing.

The very respect in which the Irish harp was held led to its downfall in a way. From the Middle Ages until the end of the seventeenth century, harp music and the harp itself remained unchanged. Then came the harsh, anti-Catholic laws of the seventeenth and eighteenth centuries. Many wealthy Catholic families left the country. This robbed the harpists of much of their audience. At the same time Italian music, with its pleasing harmonies, was becoming known in Ireland.

Many people liked the new, melodic music better than the long, drawn-out chords of the Irish harp. Gradually harp music lost its standing.

The poet Yeats once said that beautiful old Irish tunes are really fairy music picked up by eavesdroppers. One such eavesdropper, Yeats said, was the blind O'Carolan, the last of the great Irish harpists. According to Yeats, O'Carolan once slept on a fairy mound. Ever afterward fairy tunes ran in his head.

O'Carolan died in 1738, and after his time the fiddle took the place of the harp.

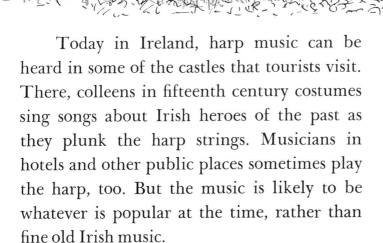

Today in Ireland, harp music can be heard in some of the castles that tourists visit. There, colleens in fifteenth century costumes sing songs about Irish heroes of the past as they plunk the harp strings. Musicians in hotels and other public places sometimes play the harp, too. But the music is likely to be whatever is popular at the time, rather than fine old Irish music.

Today the harp appears on Irish coins and on some of the Irish flags. It is seen in the national coat of arms, the presidential flag, as well as in the royal arms of the United Kingdom.

A symbol of sorrow as well as of joy, nothing could be more appropriate for St. Patrick's Day than the harp.

Pipe and Fiddle

Good sir, pray I thee
For of Saint Charite
Come and dance with me
   in Ireland.
     —From a fourteenth century dance song

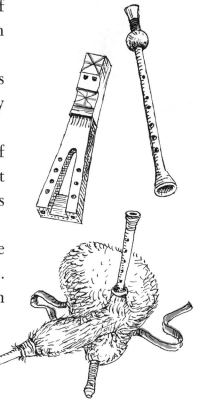

Among the motifs on St. Patrick's Day party napkins and greeting cards are dancing couples, circles of dancers, pipers, and fiddlers. For the Irish have long loved dancing. And for a long time, they have danced to the music of pipe and fiddle.

Today pipers and fiddlers are an important part of St. Patrick's Day celebrations in the United States. In parades, bands of pipers, some of them dressed in kilts, march to the wail of bagpipes.

Fiddlers who know Irish reels and jigs are in great demand for St. Patrick's Day dances and entertainments.

The reed pipe is one of the oldest of musical instruments. According to ancient myths, it was invented by the god Pan, who is usually pictured with a pipe in his hand.

Irish stone carvings of St. Patrick's time show people playing reed pipes or bagpipes. In those days a simple reed pipe was the main source of music for most people. A chieftain or rich man might have a piper as well as a harper as part of his household. A piper of this sort probably played the bagpipe.

It is thought that Celtic tribes from the Middle East brought the bagpipe to the British Isles. There, people living in what is now Scotland made it their chief instrument. It may be that the Irish found out about it from these Scottish people.

Like the Scottish, the Irish used the bagpipe as a marching pipe. Its shrill, nasal wail aroused their courage in battle, served as an alarm, and called scattered soldiers together.

As time went on, the Irish improved on the simple bagpipe. By the late 1500s, it was becoming more like the soft Irish pipes of later times. The Uillean or "elbow" pipe that is heard today sounds something like an oboe.

Uillean pipe

In the eighteenth century, an outstanding Irish piper named Talbot was ordered to play for the British king. The same piper once said, "My music is for the ears, not the heels." He refused to play for dancing.

At that time, ordinary pipers played for pennies in barns or at crossroads—wherever people gathered on a Saturday night for a *ceili*. At a ceili, hardworking people danced their cares away in the fast tempo of jigs and reels. They also sang songs and listened to stories.

74

Fiddlers played dance music, too, and like pipers, they made a living as best they could.

Sometimes a pastor disapproved of things that went on at a ceili. Then the fiddler or piper would be blamed for stirring people up with his music.

Poorly paid, condemned by the clergy, a fiddler or piper had no reason to rejoice in his lot. In time fiddling and piping were left mostly to the lame and the blind. Pipers and fiddlers were thought of as beggars.

Then came the years of famine in the nineteenth century, when thousands fled or left Ireland. For half a century, gloom hung over the country. There was little heart for music and dancing. Crushed by hardship under British rule, the Irish had lost their pride. They saw no value in their own language, music, or dances.

With the twentieth century, came the revival of interest in everything Irish. Native songs and dances, Irish pipes and fiddles came into their own again.

On this side of the Atlantic, many people knew only sentimental Irish songs like *Mother Machree* or *When Irish Eyes Are Smiling*. Then in the 1960s, young Irish-Americans discovered true Irish songs.

A jig called *The Irish Washerwoman* was perhaps the one well-known Irish dance tune. Actually there are hundreds and hundreds of jigs. There are also countless reels, hornpipes, flings, marches, and plenty of slow airs.

Today, traditional Irish music is heard in the United States more and more, not only on St. Patrick's Day but all year-round. Groups of musicians, some of them straight from Ireland, go on concert tours. Some record their music in Irish albums.

Nor are the colorful rhythms confined to fiddle and pipes. It is now the custom to include the accordion, the tin whistle, the concertina, the Irish harp, and the *bodhran and bones*. The bodhran is a flat, goatskin drum. "Bones" is the double-ended drumstick used to beat it.

Around St. Patrick's Day, Irish musical groups are in great demand. So are Irish folk dancers, harpists, fiddlers, pipers, and singers.

Alongside the professional performers, Irish Americans young and old enjoy singing Irish songs and doing Irish dances. While some are beginners, others are old timers, handing down what they know to keep it from being lost.

Top Hats, Clay Pipes, and Petticoats

Another cheerful St. Patrick's Day symbol in the United States is an Irishman wearing a top hat and swinging a cane. He may be dancing or not, but the look on his face is sure to be good-humored.

It used to be that a black woman was almost always shown in pictures or on the stage as a "mammy." Her head was done up in a bandana, her face wreathed in smiles.

In the same way, an Irishman almost always was pictured as a carefree, happy-go-lucky person. With his battered stove pipe hat and tattered coattails, he usually seemed to be a kind of comic.

The people who fled from Ireland to keep from starving were often tattered, it is true. But they were seldom like the comic figure of stage and story.

Sometimes the top-hatted figure in St. Patrick's Day party decorations is swinging his partner in a jig or reel. Sometimes he is by a fireside, smoking a pipe of the same Irish clay of which his cottage is built.

The "best" clothes of the Irish country-man did include a jaunty hat with a high crown that sloped outward to a narrow brim. The countryman would also wear a white stock, a vest, cutaway jacket, and white socks below tight knee britches.

Women and girls wore dark head shawls, light blouses, and long, full skirts over several petticoats.

In St. Patrick's Day greeting cards and party decorations, the styles may be right, but the garments, even the top hats, are usually colored green in the spirit of the Irish holiday.

Leprechauns

Do you not catch the tiny clamour,
Busy click of an Elfin hammer,
Voice of the Leprechaun singing shrill,
As he merrily plies his trade?
—From *The Leprechaun: or Fairy Shoemaker*
by William Allingham

One of the most appealing of St. Patrick's Day symbols is the tiny shoemaker known to us as the leprechaun. Almost everyone has met the wizened, bearded dwarf in Irish folk or fairy tales. In his green suit and cap, he adds one more sprightly touch to the Irish holiday.

The little shoemaker is one of a whole horde of Irish fairies. More vivid and lifelike than many other kinds, Irish fairies are divided into two classes. There are the trooping fairies who live and travel in groups, and the solitary fairies who live alone. Trooping fairies are usually kind and pleasant. Solitary ones like the leprechaun are mostly mean and spiteful.

One of the few industrious fairies, the leprechaun works day and night mending the shoes of other fairies, whose chief delights are music and dancing.

80

The little leprechauns were not always solitary or even shoemakers. Long, long ago, they were part of a group known as *Luchorpan,* meaning the wee ones. Somehow, through the years, the name luchorpan became confused with an Irish word meaning one-shoemaker. Since shoemakers usually lived alone and were considered grumpy, the leprechaun became a loner. And he was usually described as working on a single shoe, rather than on a pair.

The leprechauns in most stories are rich and bad-tempered. They prefer to live far from the homes of human beings. If you capture one and keep your eye on him, he cannot vanish. He might even tell you where his pot of gold is buried, for this is what he uses as ransom. But a leprechaun can never be trusted. Somehow they always manage to get away without paying.

In one well-known tale, a leprechaun captured in a field said that his gold was buried under a certain weed. The man who had caught him tied his red handkerchief to the weed, then went off to get his shovel. When he came back, the leprechaun had outwitted him. On every single weed the man found a red handkerchief.

The Irish were always in awe of their fairies. They believed that fairies sometimes kidnapped brides and snatched babies from their cradles. A person enticed into a fairy mound might be kept there for a hundred years, they thought. Listening to fairy music could make a man or woman lose all sense of human care or joy. Forever afterward, he or she would seem to live in another world. Such a person might become a seer, a great poet, or musician. The harpist O'Carolan is said to have gathered all his lovely tunes while sleeping on a fairy *rath*.

Known also as fairy forts or fairy mounds, raths are small fields encircled by ditches or walls made of sod or stone. They may have been ancient forts, ancient sheepfolds, or small farmsteads. Some of the fairy raths can still be seen in Ireland to this day. And many Irish farmers will not disturb them any more than they will interfere with trees or paths that are thought to belong to fairies.

Where did the Irish fairies come from? Some scholars believe that they were the gods of ancient Ireland. When the Christian god took their places, these scholars say, they dwindled in size in people's imaginations to the tiny beings they are today.

Of all the many Irish fairies, only the solitary little leprechaun has a place in St. Patrick's Day. Who knows why? Because he is usually described as wearing green? If so, this is ironic. For the leprechaun's green clothes were meant to blend with the green of nature, leaving him unnoticed!

Among the souvenir figurines for St. Patrick's Day and on many holiday greeting cards is a cheery, fat-bellied little old man dressed mostly in green. Part leprechaun, part Irish farmer, he is what we might call a manufactured symbol of the Irish holiday.

Poteen and Potatoes

Like most holidays, St. Patrick's Day has its special foods and goodies. At home, many Irish-Americans enjoy traditional dishes. Corned beef and cabbage, mulligatawny soup, Irish stew, and Irish soda bread are all popular. The same dishes are a holiday feature in many restaurants.

A lucky few may be treated by an Irish cook to a delicious dish known as colcannon. Mashed potatoes are combined with shredded kale or cabbage, minced onion, and melted butter to make this classic Irish dish.

The St. Patrick's Day spirit that colors everything possible a vivid green extends even to bakeries and candy counters. There we find green cookies and candies, green icing, green ice cream and cake.

Most people were too poor to do much feasting in Ireland itself during much of the time that St. Patrick's Day has been celebrated there. Those who were better off used to brew ale in February and keep it for St. Patrick's Day. On the holiday, family and friends had pickled salmon and oaten bread along with the ale.

In the evening, the men gathered at inns and public houses to "drown the shamrock." They wished one another good luck, good health, and low rents. With the toasts, they drank St. Patrick's Pot or Poteen, a whiskey made from potatoes.

The famous Irish white potato first grew in Peru, in South America. Brought to Europe by Spanish explorers, potatoes are said to have washed up on Irish shores from wrecks of the Spanish Armada in 1588.

Like the tomato and eggplant, the potato is part of the nightshade family of plants. Since some of these are deadly, the potato, like the other two vegetables, was looked on with suspicion at first.

People remarked that the potato grew from an "eye" or bud instead of a seed like other plants that were good to eat. The bumpy, irregular shape of potatoes seemed suspicious, too.

When distrust gave way to curiosity, people discovered that potatoes tasted good and were very filling.

Ireland was the first country in Europe to grow potatoes on a large scale. There, the coming of the *prata* or potato in the seventeenth century seemed a blessing at first. Not only was the potato tasty, it was easy to grow and to cook. Grain had to be cut, threshed, and ground into meal. Potatoes, on the other hand, were easy to dig and could simply be boiled or roasted in a fire.

Most Irish farm families had only a few acres of rented land. They had to feed and clothe themselves and pay the rent with what they raised. The money they got for their butter or grain might pay the rent. The fleece from their few sheep might bring enough to pay for clothing. Potatoes were a welcome new source of food.

A family of six could feed itself for a year on an acre and a half of potatoes. Eaten together with milk and butter, the potato was fairly nourishing. For many Irish people, it became almost the sole diet.

Until the middle of the 1800s, it was the Irish custom to marry early. A girl was often only sixteen, the boy she married a year older. Usually the couple produced a large family. By 1840, there were more than 8,000,000 people in Ireland.

A few years later, a plant disease attacked the Irish potato crop. The blight, bad enough in 1845, reached its peak in 1846 and 1847. During the famine years, a million Irish died of starvation or from disease caused by lack of enough food. Another million left the country.

Today, in Ireland, farmers spray their potato plants against the deadly fungus.

It is said that potatoes came to the United States from England by way of Bermuda in 1621 and were planted in Virginia. Scottish-Irish immigrants brought them to Londonderry, New Hampshire, in 1719. Soon after that, they became known as the Irish potato.

> Sublime potatoes! that, from Antrim's
>   shore
> To famous Kerry, form the poor man's
>   store;
> Agreeing well with every place and
>   state—
> The peasant's noggin, or the rich man's
>   plate.
>
> —From *Popular Songs of Ireland*
> Compiled by Thomas Crofton Croker

St. Patrick's Day Parades

In Dublin or New York City, in Seattle or Sydney, in Boston or Montreal, people of Irish blood march in parades on St. Patrick's Day. People who are not Irish often march with their Irish friends. Others stand on the sidelines to watch, for St. Patrick's Day parades are seldom dull.

When the first one took place in the American colonies is hard to say. Some claim that it was in New York City during the American Revolution. One March 17th, they say, four hundred Irish soldiers of the British army marched up Broadway from the waterfront. At the end of their march, they were served a banquet. The British army had supplied a fife-and-drum band as well as the banquet. Knowing how the Irish felt about British rule, the army was hoping to bribe them. As it turned out, soon afterward the four hundred Irish soldiers all deserted and joined the American army.

By the 1850s, a St. Patrick's Day parade was held every year in Boston, Philadelphia, Atlanta, Cleveland, and many other cities. By the 1870s, there were enough Irish in Los Angeles to make it an annual event there.

88

Today, there are St. Patrick's Day parades in at least thirty of the fifty states. The largest and grandest is in New York City. Only the Russian May Day parade in Moscow is larger.

Beginning at noon, more than 100,000 marchers parade up Fifth Avenue in New York City, a mile or two beyond St. Patrick's Cathedral. For six hours or more the parade continues past cheering throngs.

Band after band passes by, many of them from schools and colleges in New York or in other states. There are fife-and-drum corps, as well as regular marching bands or musicians dressed in kilts, playing bagpipes. The air rings with the rhythms of lively marching tunes and Irish favorites like *Danny Boy, The Minstrel Boy,* or *Garryowen.*

Dignitaries in morning coats and top hats wear sashes of green, white, and orange. Usually they carry a blackthorn shillelagh or walking stick. Members of the fire, police, sanitation, and other city departments march in contingent. Many have their own bands.

At times the parade becomes a sea of swirling batons, waving pompoms, pennants, and banners. Some of the banners bear the names of counties in Ireland—Cork, Kerry, and others. Some have the names of Irish clans or families—the Flanagans, the Murphys, or the McGillicuddys.

There are always novelties among the marchers—a horse that someone has painted green, a man with green eyebrows and mustache, a woman with green shamrocks on her face. Each year brings something different.

Everywhere, among the marchers and spectators alike, there are green hats, green banners, and green carnations. And whether they are Irish or not, almost everybody is smiling.

The New York St. Patrick's Day parade was not always such a happy occasion. There were times in the nineteenth century when the marchers were insulted, pelted with rocks, even beaten by bystanders. During the 1890s, the line of march led past factories and employment offices with signs that said, "No Irish need apply."

Today, onlookers at the New York City parade find it easy to believe that there are more people of Irish origin in the United States than there are in Ireland. It is easier still when they remember that this is only one of the many parades taking place in towns and cities throughout the nation.

In Ireland itself, people watch the New York parade on the evening television news. They also watch parades held in other parts

of their own country, for, although the holiday is celebrated more quietly in Ireland, there are parades of some kind nearly everywhere.

In larger centers like Galway in western Ireland, city officials march in regalia. Pupils from schools of Irish dancing march proudly in Celtic costume. Veterans of the old Irish Republican Army display their medals. The bands play tunes of rebel songs from the nation's past. Instead of standing on the sidelines, many citizens, young and old, join the procession, too. The main parade in Galway is followed later in the day by a colorful military parade.

In Dublin, Ireland's capital, there is also a large military parade on St. Patrick's Day. The Irish flags and banners furnish touches of green. Aside from these, there is no emphasis on the color green in the Dublin parade, though. Since everyone is Irish, there is no need for it.

In the United States, which is made up of people from many lands, it is not enough to be simply a part of the blend that we call American. Each ethnic group needs something to set it apart and to keep alive its own traditions.

92

For Irish-Americans, the celebration of St. Patrick's Day helps serve this purpose. The parades and parties, the display of green, and the symbols like harps, shamrocks, and shillelaghs serve another purpose, too. They are reminders that all of us, except the American Indians, were at one time or another newcomers to these shores.

Stories for St. Patrick's Day

Boden, Alice. *A Field of Buttercups.* New York: Henry Z. Walck & Co., Inc., 1974. A leprechaun story in picture book form for younger children.

Colum, Padraic. *The King of Ireland's Son.* New York: The Macmillan Company, 1967. Adventures that draw on centuries of Irish folklore.

Danaher, Kevin. *Folktales of the Irish Countryside.* New York: David White, 1970. Tales of Irish giants, ghosts, fairies, fools, and kings, as Kevin Danaher of Dublin heard them many years ago.

Dobrin, Arnold. *Gilly Gilhooly: A Tale of Ireland.* New York: Crown Publishers, Inc., 1976. An amusing picture/story book for younger children.

Haviland, Virginia. *Favorite Fairy Tales Told in Ireland.* Boston: Little, Brown and Company, 1961. Five lively stories, suitable for elementary school children.

Jacobs, Joseph, ed. *Celtic Fairy Tales.* London: The Bodley Head, 1970. Contains the forty-seven stories of the two original Jacobs collections.

Jacobs, Joseph. *Hudden and Dudden, and Donald O'Neary.* New York: Coward, 1968. A picture story book with text from Jacobs' *Celtic Fairy Tales.* Good for story hour or for reading alone.

Janice. Illustrated by Mariana. *Little Bear Marches in the St. Patrick's Day Parade.* New York: Lothrop, Lee & Shepard Co., 1967. Amusing picture/story book for younger children.

Lynch, Patricia. *Brogeen and the Bronze Lizard.* New York: The Macmillan Company, 1952. The adventures of a warmhearted leprechaun who befriends two lonely children.

Lynch, Patricia. *Brogeen Follows the Magic Tune.* New York: The Macmillan Company, 1954. Brogeen gets into trouble by taking a lonely fiddler into a fairy fort. Both the above are suitable for reading aloud in installments.

Pilkington, R. M. *Shamrock and Spear: Tales and Legends from Ireland*. New York: Holt, Rinehart, and Winston, Inc., 1968. For children of upper elementary school age.

McManus, Seumas. *Hibernian Nights*. New York: The Macmillan Company, 1963. In McManus's words, "the cream of my story lore," told in the style of the traditional Irish storyteller. Intricate plots. Suitable for upper elementary grades.

Stephens, James. *Irish Fairy Tales*. New York: The Macmillan Company, 1968. For children of about 9 and up.

Sources

Butler, Alban. *Lives of the Saints*. Beverly Hills, Calif.: Benziger, Inc., 1926.

Chambers, Robert, editor. *Book of Days*. Detroit: Gale Research Company, 1967 [Repr. of 1886 ed.].

Colum, Padraic, editor. *A Treasury of Irish Folklore*. New York: Crown Publishers, Inc., 1967.

Croker, Crofton T., and Clifford, Sigerson. *Legends of Kerry*. Dublin, Ireland: The Geraldine Press, 1972.

Cushing, Richard J. *St. Patrick and the Irish*. Boston: Daughters of St. Paul, 1963.

Delaney, Mary Murray. *Of Irish Ways*. Minneapolis: Dillon Press, Inc., 1973.

Irish Tourist Board. New York City Office. Brochures, pamphlets, and pictorial materials.

McManus, Seumas. *The Story of the Irish Race*. New York: The Devin-Adair Co., 1921.

McNally, S. J., Robert. *Old Ireland*. New York: Fordham University Press, 1965.

O'Brien, Máire and Conor Cruise. *A Concise History of Ireland*. New York: Beekman House, 1972.

———. *The Story of Ireland*. New York: The Viking Press, 1972.

Weiser, Francis X. *The Holyday Book*. New York: Harcourt, Brace and Company, 1956.

Yeats, W. B., editor. *Fairy and Folk Tales of Ireland*. New York: The Macmillan Company, 1973.

Index